150 years of VICTOR HARBOR HISTORY in Many Pictures with some Words

Compiled by Jeanette Bartlett

First published January 1982
© Jeanette Bartlett
All Rights Reserved
ISBN 0 9593636 0 2

Revised edition August 1992
1000 copies reprinted for the National Trust,
Victor Harbor Branch, underwritten by the
Victor Harbor Rotary Club, with a substantial gift.

Designed by Ainslie Roberts

Wholly set, printed and bound by
Gillingham Printers Pty Ltd
Adelaide, South Australia.

Preface

In April, 1982, it will be the 180th anniversary since the meeting in Encounter Bay, in 1802, between Captain Matthew Flinders and Commander Nicolas Baudin.

It will also be the 145th anniversary in April since Captain Crozier, in HMS 'Victor', named Victor Harbor after his ship.

To commemorate these two historic events, a Heritage Festival will be held from 24 April to 2 May, 1982.

The district has a unique place in history. Not only can it lay claim to being, in 1802, the birthplace of South Australia, but Governor Hindmarsh nearly succeeded in establishing the Capital of the State where Victor Harbor now stands.

This book is a pictorial record of interesting and significant events, from 1802 when Encounter Bay was named by Captain Matthew Flinders, to the arrival of the first permanent white settlers, through to present day Victor Harbor. We have gathered what we could of the evidence that still remains of those humble beginnings by the pioneers of the district—those who laid the foundation stones for the development of the Victor Harbor area.

So many people have responded to our call for Heritage material for this book that it would be impossible to list them all. We trust that this collective 'thank you' will express our appreciation. Those who have made outstanding contributions are listed on our 'thank you' page at the back of this book.

What has emerged from our research, though, is significant. We have found an overwhelming enthusiasm and an awareness of Heritage in everyone contacted, often by people we had thought would not be all that interested. It has brought us to the conviction that if there is a common bond that can knit a community together to the exclusion of all differences, then that bond is an awareness of the need for Heritage—a feeling for our past history that will help us face the future with greater insight and confidence.

This small book contains many sins of omission — material we know to be somewhere, but have not been able to trace. We would be grateful to receive any corrections, illustrations, or forgotten pieces of our history that will help to make future printings of this book more comprehensive.

Mrs Jeanette Bartlett
Victor Harbor

'Le Geographe' and 'The Investigator'. Captain Matthew Flinders, R.N. at left. Plaque shown below is on a granite boulder at the summit of Rosetta Head (The Bluff).

IN COMMEMORATION OF THE MEETING NEAR THIS BLUFF BETWEEN H.M.S. 'INVESTIGATOR'—MATTHEW FLINDERS WHO EXPLORED THE COAST OF SOUTH AUSTRALIA AND M.F. 'LE GEOGRAPHE'—NICOLAS BAUDIN, APRIL 8. 18⬦ ON BOARD THE 'INVESTIGATOR' WAS JOHN FRANKLIN THE ARCTIC DISCOVERER. THESE ENGLISH AND FRENCH EXPLOR⬦ HELD FRIENDLY CONFERENCE. AND FLINDERS NAMED THE PLACE OF MEETING.'ENCOUNTER BAY'.

UNVEILED BY HIS EXCELLENCY LORD TENNYSON.
APRIL 8, 1902.

Ceremony on 8 April 1902 to unveil plaque to commemorate the meeting in Encounter Bay between Captain Matthew Flinders and Commander Nicolas Baudin, one hundred years earlier. Lord Tennyson (centre) and Simpson Newland (reading) beside him. *(Below)* Pioneers of the District at the same ceremony.

The events

1802	Encounter Bay discovered and named by Captain Matthew Flinders, commemorating his encounter in the bay with the French Commander, Nicolas Baudin, of the ship 'Le Geographe', approximately 11 miles south-east of the Murray Mouth on 8th April.
1829	Sealers reported the existence of Lake Alexandrina.
1831	Captain Collet Barker and his party, travelled along the Bay to the Murray Mouth, where he was speared by Aborigines on Younghusband Peninsula.
1836	South Australia proclaimed a colony. Colonel Light's choice of Adelaide as the site for the capital was unsuccessfully opposed by Governor Hindmarsh, who preferred Encounter Bay.
1837	Captain R. Crozier, anchoring in the lee of Granite Island, gave to the adjacent part of the mainland the name of his ship 'Victor'. Two whaling stations established, the first in March near Granite Island, the second at the Bluff in April. Captain Blenkinsopp, Manager of the whaling station, piloted Captain Crozier to his anchorage. Blenkinsopp and his party drowned at the Murray Mouth in December. His body was recovered and buried in his garden. First export from South Australia, 150 barrels of whale oil. 236 ton barque 'South Australian', loading cargo in the lee of the Bluff, broke her moorings in a violent gale from the south-east, hit Black Reef, scraped across it and was blown ashore to become a total loss. The 337 ton 'Solway' moored near the Bluff dragged her anchor in another south-easterly gale and was wrecked on Black Reef also. During the same gale, the 105 ton 'John Pirie', anchored near the 'Solway', broke loose and was blown shorewards. Her Captain hoisted sail, drove her over Black Reef close to Wright Island and beached her on shore. She was later refloated.
1838	Good anchorage reported at Victor Harbor. Port of Victor Harbor proclaimed on 26th June. First vessel to load a cargo of whale oil, in the lee of Granite Island, was the 'Goshawk' in August.
1839	Rev. R.W. Newland and his party of 30 arrived at Encounter Bay to become the first permanent white settlers. Governor Gawler suggests that vessels be sent direct from England to Encounter Bay. Land subdivided into 134 acre lots, selling for £1 per acre.

1840   Exports from South Australia included 536 barrels of black oil, 158 barrels of sperm oil, 8 casks of seal skins and 655 bundles of whale bone.

The Bluff, as it has been known since earliest times, officially named Rosetta Head by Governor Gawler in honour of the wife of George Fife Angas.

South Australian Company suffered a loss of £50,000. It withdrew from Encounter Bay and sold its share in the whaling stations to Hack & Co.

1843   First permanent Police Station established at Policeman's Point, near the present-day Causeway.

1846   First church built – The Tabernacle, measuring 28 ft. x 19 ft., with a verandah on both sides. It was built of limestone and mortar and was first lit by whale oil lamps and tallow candles. It was in use until 1873.

1847   Road from Adelaide to Victor Harbor via Port Elliot opened.

First hotel opened – The Fountain Inn at Yilki. It was also the venue for early District Council meetings.

The cutter 'Alpha' sank at Rosetta Head during a storm. She was laden with bricks and sank in nine fathoms. Refloated and offered for sale 12 months later.

1852   Cutter 'Jane & Emma' ran ashore on the Bluff, total wreck.

1853   Road connecting Victor Harbor and Goolwa opened.

First meeting of District Council of Encounter Bay.

1854   The foreshore road and the Bluff Jetty built, without the consent of the owner of the land, for use by the whaling trade. John Hindmarsh sued the District Council for £48,180 – later settled for £2,000

Port Elliot selected as the port for the Murray trade.

Completion of the railway between Goolwa and Port Elliot.

Wright Is." John Pirie"
and Rosetta Head
1837

Ainslie Roberts
1972

1857	Accurate survey made for most suitable place for moorings to be laid down.
1859	After several shipping disasters at Port Elliot, site of the port was moved to Victor Harbor.
1860	Gradual collapse of market for whale oil and whalebone due to competition from mineral oils and the change in fashions.
1861	Victor established as a port, anchorage for all vessels. Brig 'Content' loaded Milang wheat at Victor Harbor. The Captain spoke highly of the port.
1862	Government laying down strong moorings. Contract let for £8,500 for building the jetty and pier on 25th June, and jetty commenced. Jetty out 640 feet from land.
1863	Victor Harbour did not exist as a town before this time. Large stone buildings constructed and licensed. Later known as Victor Harbor House. Built to provide accommodation for workmen constructing the jetty. Small coasters begin to call regularly. Road connecting Yankalilla opened. Jetty out 700 feet. Meeting at Port Elliot urging the extension of jetty to Granite Island. Bridges over the Hindmarsh and Inman Rivers opened and town begins to develop after being surveyed by J. L. Hyndman. Jetty works proceeding.
1864	Grades eased on the hill out of the town on the Yankalilla road. Railway extension from Port Elliot to Victor Harbor opened, followed by the opening of the jetty, named 'Victoria Pier'. Port Elliot proved unsuitable as an anchorage. Dinner given by Mr. Matthews, builder of the jetty. Goods shed built. First schooner to arrive direct from overseas.
1865	Schooner 'Gem' brought telegraph poles from Fremantle, W.A. Crown Hotel built and licensed. First bank – Bank of South Australia opened, later taken over by Union Bank.
1866	First vessel to sail from Victor Harbor direct to overseas destination. Cut Hill Road opened. Potatoes bought in from Warrnambool. Harbor enlarged by proclamation and renamed Port Victor. First vessel to discharge cargo at the port. Phillip Wheaton opened the first General Store (1866-1891).
1867	Telegraph Station built. Cobb & Co's coach on the run from Adelaide. Fare 14/6d. single, 7¾ hour journey. Contract signed with Jabez Grimble for building Cut Hill stone wall. Two barques arrive direct from London. Deputation to the Commissioner of Public Works urging an extension of the jetty to Granite Island. Tannery established to tan leather.

1868   Reports a number of large buildings in the town.
Cut Hill stone wall completed.
Contract signed for the construction of the lifeboat shed.
Foundation stone laid for Newland Memorial Church.
First Harbourmaster appointed, Mr. R.B. Williams, at an annual salary of £200.

1869   Railway to Strathalbyn completed.

1870/1 Two large wool stores erected by the railway line in the town.
St. Augustines Church commenced.
Whaling revived, but short lived.

1872   Last whale caught by Mr. Ranford and towed to the Bluff.
Blacksmith's shop and sleeping accommodation erected on Granite Island.

1874   First licensed school on site of present St. John Centre, known as Alexandra Cottage, operated by a Mr. William S. Evans.

1875   Causeway extended to Island.

1877   Primary School opened in Torrens Street.

1878   Work commenced on building the Screwpile Jetty and the Breakwater – 1,000 ft. long.
Four ships reported loading in the port at once.

1879   Piles and timber for the Screwpile Jetty arrive.

1880   Mount Breckan built, consisting of 22 rooms with 80 foot tower.

1881   First vessel to use the Screwpile Jetty, coastal steamer 'Penola' in November, loading 260 bales of wool.
Austral Hotel licensed, later became Pipiriki Guest House, demolished in the 1970's.

1882	Breakwater construction completed. 200,000 tons of rock used to build breakwater, taken out of the Island in seven blasts. 300 tons of fencing wire unloaded for Murray settlers.
1883	Several large ships loading wool at a rate of 1,250 bales per day. First light on end of breakwater, kerosene operated. Contract for the construction of the first stage of Parliament House led to quarry operations beginning on the northern side of West Island. Work on the granite basement of Parliament House was in progress until 1885 when a dispute caused work to be suspended. 12,000 cub. feet quarried in first stage.
1884	Breakwater light altered to burn gas. Strathalbyn railway line connected with the main line at Mount Barker junction. House purchased on Granite Island for the Harbourmaster, built in 1870's. Salvation Army opened.
1885	Railway to Victor Harbor converted to steam traction.
1888	Permit granted to District Council of Encounter Bay to plant trees on Granite Island.
1891	David Bell took over Phillip Wheaton's General Store.
1892	First lighthouse operated from Granite Island. Five street lights needing a lamplighter.
1893	Mine props shipped to Moonta.
1894	Horse drawn tram commenced running to Granite Island. Tim Mahoney first to drive tram.
1896	Grosvenor Hotel built.
1902	Plaque unveiled by His Excellency Lord Tennyson at Summit of the Bluff to commemorate the historic meeting between Captain Matthew Flinders and Commander Nicolas Baudin on 8th April, 1802.
1904/5	Victor Harbor Town Hall built.
1906	Watsons Gap Bridge replaced (original timber one built in 1863).
1907	First express train, Adelaide to Victor Harbor.
1909	Mount Breckan burnt – in ruins.
1910	Small locomotives permitted to work between Port Victor and Granite Island. Island placed under control of Railways Department. Victor Harbor High School classes commenced. Decline of the port apparent. The kiosk on Granite Island built for £650.
1911	Skipper of barque 'Margit' disappeared without trace. 'Margit's' first mate appointed Captain, ship taken to sea and ran aground near the Coorong.
1912	Victor Harbor Times published its first newspaper. Police Station near causeway demolished. HMAS Destroyers at Victor – first R.A.N. ships.
1913	Mount Breckan rebuilt.
1914	Corporation of the Town of Victor Harbor proclaimed. Mount Breckan re-opened its doors as a Guest House.

1916	Reservoir on the River Hindmarsh commenced. Dredge 'Adelaide' working in the port, deepening sections of harbour.
1917	Reservoir opened at a cost of £69,000 with a capacity of 130,000 gallons. Soliders' Memorial Gardens established.
1919	'Delco' electric light plant installed. Annexe added to Newland Church.
1920	First plane to visit Victor Harbor – Captain Harry Butler on 1st January.
1921	Barque 'Eugene Schneider' on way to Victor Harbor to pick up cargo of wheat. French Captain misread map and nearly lost ship at Port Victoria. Post Office in Ocean Street completed.
1923	E.S. & A. Bank opened for business. New oval comprising 14 acres opened.
1924	Electric light first used on causeway to Granite Island during Christmas week. Largest vessel to anchor in the harbour, HMS 'Hood', weighing 42,000 tons, together with HMS 'Repulse' and five other warships.
1925	Victor Harbor Steam Laundry was first established in town, opened in January. Lifeboat 'Arthur Searcy' stationed at Victor Harbor was in use between 1925-1941. The first Anzac Bridge built and opened across the River Inman.

(Below) Section of a diary written on Christmas Day, 1850.

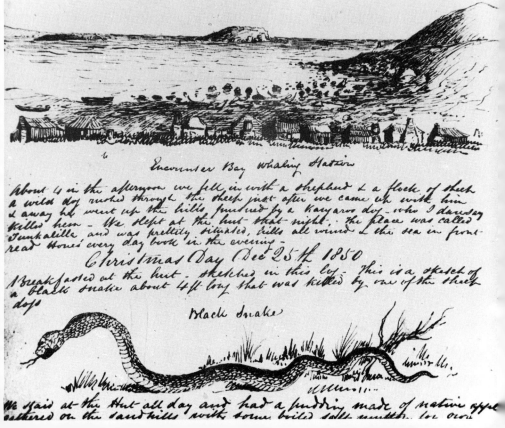

1927	Second Congregational Church in Victoria Street completed.
1928	Road to Adelaide bitumenised.
	Commercial Bank opened (new premises in 1930).
	Victor Harbor Carnival, week long festivities held to raise funds to further upgrade existing foreshore amenities.
	Savings Bank opened.
1929	South Coast District Hospital opened.
1930	Church of Christ opened.
1931	Horse drawn Passenger Car No. 7 withdrawn from use.
	First boat used by Victor Harbor Sea Scouts – The Lady Hore-Ruthven, whose husband was Chief Scout between 1927-34.
1936	Three hotels, thirty-six guest houses, bowling greens, croquet lawns, tennis courts, golf links, boats for hire on river or sea, racing club, dance palais, picture theatres, public baths, rifle range, all well established.
	Trains running daily from Adelaide to Victor.
	State Centenary Celebrations held in Victor Harbor, shops gaily decorated.
	Victor Harbor Grand Prix held in December attracting approximately 40,000 spectators.
1937	To commemorate the naming of the harbor by Captain R. Crozier, who entered the Harbor on 26th April 1837 in his ship HMS 'Victor', a plaque was unveiled by Dr. Grenfell Price on Granite Island.
1938	The Bluff and the surroundings declared a recreation reserve and placed under the control of the Encounter Bay District Council.
1946	Mount Breckan used for a Post War Rehabilitation Hospital.
1948	Victor Harbor Trotting Club opened.
1952	First shop built at Harbor Traders.
1955	Public baths demolished.
1956	Victor Harbor Yacht Club established.
1957	Harbor Traders Shopping Complex completed – 17 shops.
1958	Miss Victor Harbor Quest held on the lawns.
	ETSA took over electricity supply.
1959	Margaret Nott of Victor Harbor chosen from 10 other entrants to represent Australia in Miss World Contest. Quest held at the Swimmers' Paradise Motel, now known as the Family Inn.
	Victor Harbor Regalaires Marching Team (5 years approx.).
1960	Road to Adelaide rebuilt.
1961	New Hotel Victor rebuilt.
1962	Mount Breckan purchased by the Adelaide Bible Institute.
	Whaler's Haven Colony Museum and Settlers Cottage opened to the public.
1965	New Council Chambers opened in October.
1968	St. John Ambulance Centre opened.
1969	Summerlea Mansion demolished, replaced by the Centre Shopping Complex.
	Granite Island declared Fauna Sanctuary, Cape Barren Geese and Kangaroo Island Wallabies introduced to the Island.
	Meals-on-Wheels established at Victor Harbor.

1970	Memorial to Captain Blenkinsopp unveiled by the Governor of South Australia, Sir James Harrison.
	Proposal to close Strathalbyn-Victor Harbor railway line rejected by Public Works Standing Committee.
	Woolworths established in Victor Harbor.
1972	An anchor, believed to be from the 'Solway', recovered from the seabed where the 'South Australian', 'Solway' and 'John Pirie' were anchored in 1937.
1976	Urimbirra Fauna Park opened in November.
	Victor Harbor Sea Rescue Squadron formed.
1981	$15,000,000 Tourist Complex, including a motel and licensed restaurant, proposed for Victor Harbor. Plan includes area between Coral Street, Flinders Parade and Pine Grove Kiosk.
	New footbridge constructed across River Inman, also named the Anzac Bridge.
1982	Heritage Festival, 24th April to 2nd May.

(Below) 1846 Water-colour of Encounter Bay by George French Angas.

CHART
OF THE ANCHORAGES IN
ENCOUNTER BAY

by Wm Light Surv.r General

South Australia.

The ground here rises all the way to the Hills, and certainly not adapted for a Capital. The banks above the beach are precipitous, and there is no fresh water within three or four miles. and that not very good *W L*

not more than 3 or 4 ships a great swell thrown in by left *Lipson KI* to be th' ocean, and it requires a fresh breezes — This on

Granite Island

The shape of this Island is by no means correct. Ionly got the bearing of the extreme points — Easterly & Westerly *W L*

Capt.n Blanche
Fishery

Well nearly dry at ...

Breakers from next ... at the ...

S.t Australian + on Shore
+ Bois on Shore
+ Buoy on

S.A. Co.y Fishery

This anchorage, I think, is not fit for anything. — *W L*

Cape Rosetta

This Cape was called Rosetta by Lord Stephens long before Capt.n Crozier went there — *W L*

Wright I.t

Scale of Miles

S. Australia N.o 1

*ree at the same time; very unsafe in Easterly winds, and always
I doubtedly bragger, only consider for a moment that this very spot, said by
'arbour in the world, is open to the deed of the whole southern
'e judgements I imagine what look of sea there must be in
'spot under the Island where 3 or 4 ships can anchor — What
'e done with ships coming from England, had this been the
They must run for Kangaroo Island and wait there until
'o her room enough in Capt. Lipson's finest harbour is
'on them — or they must put up with some inferior bank
't likely be lost altogether — W.L. —*

*ref breaks all the way from
Rock to Granite Island in blowing weather — W.L. —*

The H.M.S. "Victor".
Plaque, at left, is
located on Granite
Island.

TO COMMEMORATE
THE NAMING OF VICTOR HARBOUR BY
CAPTAIN R CROZIER WHO ENTERED
WITH H.M.S. VICTOR ON APRIL 20, 1837
ERECTED APRIL 20, 1937

(Right) Plaque in Kent Reserve, location of one of the last camping grounds of the Ramindjeri tribe of Aborigines. The Aboriginal name for Victor Harbor was 'Poltong'.

(Above) The Poole family, photographed in 1867. Below is a group with tribal decorations, shown with the Austral Hotel in the background — later to become Pipiriki Guest House.

(Above) The Bluff and Rosetta Bay with remains of Whaling Station. *(Right)* The only existing photo of the Whaling Station — it later became Hart & Co's General Store in 1857.

The Bluff Jetty, built in 1854, still in use today, mainly by jetty anglers. Wright Island in background. Below is an 1838 sketch of Rosetta Bay, showing the Whaling Station established in April of the previous year. Note Whalers' lookout on top of the Bluff.

(Above) Plaque alongside present Whaler's Inn is on the site of the old Bluff Whaling Station. Below is the plaque, by the Masonic Hall, marking the site of the opposition Whaling Station built in 1837 — two years later this Station was relocated on Granite Island.

Top photo shows Settlers Cottage, originally built by Malen Rumblelow, Junior, at Yilki. When condemned in 1959, it was rescued by the Tilbrook family, who numbered each part, dismantled it and rebuilt it at Whaler's Haven Colony Museum. Above are some of the old Whaling weapons, and relics from the past, inside the cottage.

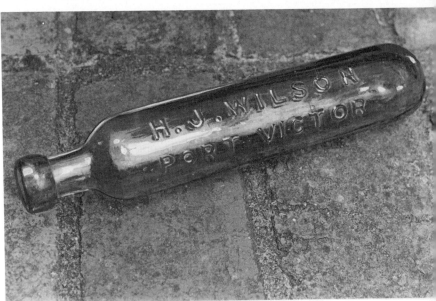

Left) Anchor recovered in Rosetta Bay from 'Solway', wrecked in 1837, now displayed at Whaler's Haven.

Right and below) Collection of relics recovered in the Bay by divers. Anchor was found at Black Reef (the Reef between Wright Island and Rosetta Bay). Brick in front of anchor is one of many from the ship 'Alpha', wrecked in 1847. An important find was the H. J. Wilson Port Victor bottle shown in foreground of lower photo.

Opposite page shows another of the rare Port Victor bottles, found in 1964 under four feet of sand while excavating for a house at Yilki.

Rev. R. W. Newland, arrived 1839. Established Churches at Yilki, Sheoak Hills, Port Elliot, Middleton, Goolwa, Hindmarsh Island, Currency Creek, Point Sturt and Milang. Also developed a stringy bark timber industry, slate works, milling and pottery industries. Was first Chairman of District Council in 1853. Known as 'Pastor of the South', he died as a result of an accident in 1864.

Below is the Tabernacle Church, built at Yilki in 1846, and a plaque and monument which mark the site today.

arly photo of the wind-powered Flour Mill. The little circular
mestone building is just west of the River Inman and has been
onverted into a home.

'Fountain Inn', first licensed premises in the area, build at Yilki in 1847. The building still stands and is used as a residence. Plaque at right is made of copper salvaged by Cain Rumbelow from the 'Solway' wreck. Below is a rear view of the Inn taken around 1870.

Eerie tales were told about Fountain Inn. Queer sounds were heard at night, like heavy feet dragging over soft sand. It was not long before rumour went around that the Inn was haunted by the ghost of a whaler, who had been injured in a drunken brawl and dragged down to the beach to die.

(Top) Rumbelow's Fishing Shed on the beach at Yilki in the 1890's. In background is the still-standing house on the corner of Ridgeway Street. Below is the General Store and Post Office established 1855, the first Post Office at Encounter Bay.

Eli King (King's Beach, west of the Bluff) bought two sections on which he built a typical crofter's cottage with boulders hauled from the Beach with horse and wooden sledge. 15 children were born to the Kings in 14 years. West Island is seen through gaps in wall in photograph showing remains of cottage in 1952. It has since been entirely restored and used as a residence.

p photo shows Petrel Cove and King's Beach today —
ng's Cottage just visible on the distant cliff top. Photo
ove is of holiday camps, early 1900's, by the road to
uff Jetty.

The Causeway began as a jetty in 1862 — was extended to Granite Island in 1875. Photo above looks across Causeway to Port Victor. Note 'pennyfarthing' bicycle — probably photographer's. Extension known as Victoria Pier, with lifeboat shed, was demolished in the 1950's. Below are the Gardens on Granite Island about the turn of the century.

Opposite page shows the old Horse Tram — loved by generations of visitors, who travelled on it to the Island and back. It was discontinued only in 1954. Bottom of page shows the Causeway today.

The Breakwater, completed in 1882 is 1,000 feet long, 30 feet wide at the top and 200 feet wide on the seabed. No granite block on its surface weighs less than 20 tons. The above photo shows what 200,000 tons of granite, gouged out of the Island by human muscle, horse-power and primitive equipment looks like today.

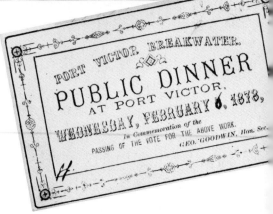

PORT VICTOR BREAKWATER.

PUBLIC DINNER
AT PORT VICTOR.

WEDNESDAY, FEBRUARY 6, 1878,

In Commemoration of the
PASSING OF THE VOTE FOR THE ABOVE WORK.
GEO. GOODWIN, Hon. Sec.

Early 1881 photo below shows Screwpile Jetty and Breakwater during construction, and Dinner Invitation of 6 February 1878.

(Above) First Jetty on Granite Island was the working Jetty, built in 1872 and later removed. Then in 1878 work started on the Screwpile Jetty (below) so called because the base of the jetty supports were threaded and screwed down into the sea-bed. It was finished in 1881.

Rockets were used to secure a line out to ships in harbour. Boatswain's chair was used to winch passengers across to Granite Island. Photos taken in 1894.

In the days when Victor Harbor was the port for much of inland Australia, these were typical of the ships that loaded the wheat and wool for overseas markets. This produce was transported by paddle steamers down the River Murray to Goolwa, then by train to Victor Harbor. For such ships, South Australia was a regular port of call up until the 1930's.

Pictured above is an early view of Victor Harbor looking towards the Bluff with the River Hindmarsh in the foreground. (Below) Victor Harbor in 1878, looking down Seaview Road. (Opposite) Looking across to Granite Island from Policeman's Point in 1879 — barge on beach at extreme left is 'John Robb', used in Breakwater construction. There were many buildings on the Island at that time.

Top of opposite page is a rare early photo taken just after the Crown
Hotel was built in 1865. View is from the beach looking up Ocean
Street with Victor Hotel on left, Crown on right, Field's Butcher Shop
in centre. Below (opposite) is a later view with Mount Breckan on sky-
line. Above is a closer look at Ocean Street (note carcasses under
verandah of Field's). Below is the same scene today.

The 'pennyfarthing' bicycles of the
1880's were the height of fashion
in transport. The height also
meant that it was a long way to
the ground if you fell off, but
these dashing Encounter Bay
enthusiasts looked confident
enough!

'Kitson' steam train crossing the Alexander Bridge, which was built over the River Hindmarsh. Bridge is still in use.

Below is the Crown Hotel, built and licensed in 1865.

Top photo shows Mrs Theisenger (centre) who conducted a business as a fruiterer for a number of years in Ocean Street. The young girl in white was Rube Lillian Theisenger, later Mrs Rube Rumbelow. Photo 1898. Above is Grosvenor's house in Ocean Street (Post Office now situated on this site).

'Adare' built by the Cudmore family in the 1890's still stands today as a monument to the past. Left, Mount Breckan, built in 1880, in ruins, February 1909. It burnt out completely in two hours. It was rebuilt in 1913; view below shows it as a Sports and Recreation Centre today.

Early view above shows Cut Hill retaining wall built by Jabez Grimble in 1868. Photo below shows the spot today. Opposite page highlights the beautiful precision workmanship in the dry stone construction, unchanged after 114 years.

Newland Memorial Church, 1869. Below shows
a wedding in the Newland Church, believed to
be in early 1900's. Annexe added to the
Church later.

The original Newland Memorial Church today is used for other
Church activities following the completion of the second one, built in
1927 and shown alongside it at left.

(Below) St. Augustines Church, built in 1870.

(Above) Wesleyan Methodist Church, built in 1865, but never completed. (Lutheran Church now stands on this site.) *(Below)* Completed in 1867, the Telegraph Station greatly improved communications between Adelaide and Victor Harbor. It is now the Postmaster's residence. Lower photo shows first permanent Police Station, built near present Causeway at Policeman's Point in 1843, demolished in 1912.

Wool Stores established near railway in 1868, used for dumping and storing wool awaiting shipment. Read's Store now used by the RSL. Bird's Butcher Shop — shown below — specialised in home deliveries. It later became 'Dalblair', is now Colonial Motel.

Robert Sweetman, Junior, tending bullock team. Railway Goods Shed, built in 1864, in background. Below is last bullock team in area, Mr. George Haskett's, in front of Hotel Victor in 1929.

In 1867 this large building and tall chimney was built as a liquid tan factory for tanning leather, demolished many years later. Toops workshop now on site. *(Below)* Hotel Grosvenor, built in 1896 with 70 rooms, A.J. Humberstone, Prop.

(Top) Erected in 1863, this was one of the first stone buildings in Victor Harbor, later known as Victor Harbor House. *(Above)* Excavation work for construction of the Hindmarsh Reservoir, completed in 1917.

Drag teams alongside the Crown Hotel, early 1900's.
Below is an early Victor Harbor football team.

(Top) Phillip Wheaton conducted the first General Store between 1866-1891. The business then taken over in 1891 by David Bell & Co. *(Above)* The same corner after 1896 with the new Hotel Grosvenor on left. *(Below)* Bell's Store today.

Southern Guest House in 1930's, now used as a Nursing Home.
Pictured below is the Clifton Guest House, built in 1908 and
standing today as a lasting memory to the times when Guest
Houses flourished in Victor Harbor.

Top picture is of 'Warringa', on the foreshore, still operating as a Guest House. Lower photo is 'Summerlea' Mansion, corner of Ocean and Coral Streets, demolished in 1969 to make way for the Centre Shopping Complex.

Post Office in Ocean Street under construction, 1921. Below is the Yilki Post Office, one of South Australia's smallest, demolished in 1976. For years a notice on the door read, 'Telegrams will not be delivered — they must be collected from this Office'!

THE RIVER INMAN
WAS CROSSED BY CAPTAIN
COLLET BARKER IN 1831 AND
WAS NAMED IN 1838, AFTER
HENRY INMAN,
FIRST INSPECTOR OF POLICE

Top photo taken in late 1920's shows mouth of River Inman. Above is the mouth of the River Hindmarsh at about the same time, when large areas of vacant land surrounded the town. Shown at left is the plaque in the Reserve by the Inman Bridge. At right is an early view of boating on the Hindmarsh, a favourite pastime enjoyed by many in the earlier years.

Photo, top of page: the Reserve
looking across to Granite Island,
late 1920's. Goods Shed and train
on left. *(above)* Flinders Parade and
Soldiers' Memorial Gardens. *(right)*
Granite Island, Station Master's
House, Wonderview Dance Palais,
Harbor Electricity Co., A. H. Land-
seer's Sheds.

Tree planting ceremony at The Bluff during World War I. Soldiers Memorial Gardens begun in 1917. Private J. McBruce was the first man from Victor Harbor killed in the Great War. *(Below)* One of many Memorial trees that commemorate those who fought for their country.

Pictured above is a view of the Gardens taken around 1930.
Picture below shows Sir Willoughby Norrie inspecting local
CMF unit on Anzac Day 1951, with Lt. P. H. Matthews.

Victor Harbor Town Band 1920, and below, Victor Harbor
Band playing at the 1979 Anzac Day Service in the
Soldiers' Memorial Gardens.

Top photo shows Bell's Corner in 1910. Car No. 71 driven by
Arthur Humberstone and No. 775 by Paul Cudmore. Lower
photo shows HMAS Destroyers at Victor Harbor in 1912. The
'Yarra', 'Parramatta' and 'Warego' became the first RAN ships.

Robert Sweetman, 1846-1933. Well known pioneer of the District. In his latter years he was often seen driving in this pony trap. Shown below is Bell's Display Cart in the 1929 Labour Day Street Procession, George Woodard and son Alan, with horse 'Gyp'.

Top of opposite page is Victor Harbor Regalaires Marching Team during Labour Day Procession, 1958, and photo below it shows an early-in-the-century Eight Hour Day March in Coral Street.

(Above) Ready to set off for a picnic in 1922. *(Below)* Victor Harbor Volunteer Fire Brigade in 1930's. Building was on reserve, opposite the Primary School. *(Lower right)* First cars travel on the new bitumen road to Victor Harbor, 1928.

1936 S.A. Centenary Grand Prix. 26 December 1936. Victor Harbor.

M.G.P. 26 December 1936. Victor Harbor.

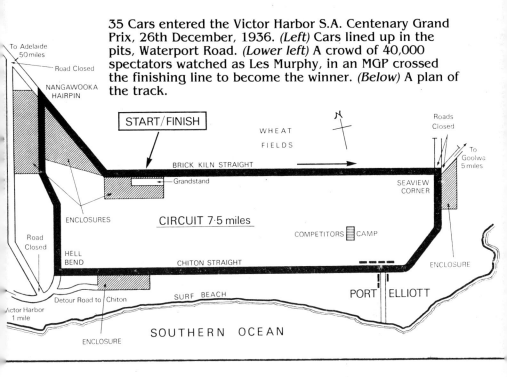

35 Cars entered the Victor Harbor S.A. Centenary Grand Prix, 26th December, 1936. *(Left)* Cars lined up in the pits, Waterport Road. *(Lower left)* A crowd of 40,000 spectators watched as Les Murphy, in an MGP crossed the finishing line to become the winner. *(Below)* A plan of the track.

To Adelaide
50 miles

Road Closed

NANGAWOOKA
HAIRPIN

START/FINISH

WHEAT
FIELDS

N

Roads
Closed

To
Goolwa
5 miles

BRICK KILN STRAIGHT

Grandstand

SEAVIEW
CORNER

ENCLOSURES

CIRCUIT 7·5 miles

COMPETITORS CAMP

Road
Closed

HELL
BEND

CHITON STRAIGHT

ENCLOSURE

Detour Road to Chiton

SURF BEACH

PORT ELLIOTT

Victor Harbor
1 mile

ENCLOSURE

SOUTHERN OCEAN

Griffins Garage (now Toop Motors) in 1930's. It is interesting to note that petrol was 2/4d. gallon.

Shops were decorated to mark the State's Centenary in
1936. Michelmore's (now Southern Bakery) and the Coffee Palace (now Spilsbury's Hardware).

Victor Harbor Primary School Fife Band, led by Captain Ron Reid,
during the State Centenary Celebrations held in the town in 1936.
Below is the South Coast District Hospital, opened in 1929.

Special Steam Train Tours to Victor Harbor, usually booked out weeks ahead, have a fascination for train enthusiasts and tourists alike. Pictured above is the '520' Victor Daylight Tour, 1978. At left, a reminder of earlier days—the '192' on its regular run to Victor Harbor in 1942.

At right is the Waterspout, 1st April 1959—it went inland over King's Beach, causing much damage before dissipating.

Victor Harbor Town Hall, built in 1904/5, in Coral Street,
Public Library alongside. Below, the first of 17 shops
completed to become Harbor Traders in 1952.

District Council of Encounter Bay, in use until new Council Chambers officially opened in 1965. Below is the present District Council of Victor Habor.

Local surfer, David Broadbent, was selected to represent Australia at the World Amateur Surfing Championships in France in September, 1980. Photo below shows yatching in the bay, a regular sight during the summer months.

Australian wildlife is at home at Urimbirra Fauna Park. The Park has had 167,500 visitors since it opened in 1976.

Trotting is a regular and long-established event—pictured below is 'Noble Peter' winning the Crown Handicap in 1950.

Annual Rotary Art Exhibition on Warland Reserve is a big Summer feature that creates keen interest. Entries are Nationwide and of a high standard. Below is the Gala Day Procession, Victor Harbor Primary School children.

Each year in January the Soldiers' Memorial Gardens and Warland Reserve come alive with the sound of laughter and Greek music at the Annual Greek Picnic. Anzac Bridge, shown below, opened in August, 1981—a combined Service Clubs Project.

Winter Clinic for 'junior' golfers conducted at the Victor
Harbor Golf Club. Shown below is the Golf Course, one of
the State's best.

Town Centre and Granite Island, 1981. And a view across to Rosetta Bay, the Bluff and Wright Island—the Catholic Church can be seen in foreground.

At left is a birds-eye view of the whole area.
Photo shows unique location of Victor Harbor—it is the only town in the State situated
between two rivers in such close proximity.'
Aerial photo *(above)* shows the Bluff and
surroundings, Wright Island on the right,
and part of the Town.

Above is Granite Island photographed from the mainland beach.
Seal Rock, shown below, is pictured from the seaward side.

The aspect of Wright Island shown above is one the visitor only sees from a boat. West Island, below, shows Petrel Cove in foreground.

(Above) Lifeboat "Arthur Searcy", used between 1925-1941.
(Below) First boat used by Victor Harbor Sea Scouts in 1931.
Purchased and named after Lady Hore Ruthven, whose
husband was Chief Scout, 1927-34.

(*above*) Some of the volunteer members of the Victor Harbor Yacht Club's Sea Rescue Squadron. Using 21 privately owned boats, they are highly trained in local navigation, radio procedure, search and rescue. The area they cover extends from south of Cape Jervis to the Murray Mouth and the extensive inland waters of the Murray, Lakes and Coorong. Working in liaison with other volunteer organisations and the Police, they provide valuable service to boating on the South Coast. (*below*) Rescue in action.

(*Opposite*) Enthusiasm, persistence and a dash of luck can often produce big surprises for amateur anglers around Victor Harbor, like the samples shown at the bottom of the page.

(*Right*) Local professional fisherman, David Jenkins displays crayfish at the opening of the season. Below is the 'Magie'—one of the many crayboats plying between Victor Harbor and the fishing grounds along the South coast.

alen Rumbelow, Murray and Lin Shannon, Bill and George Ewen,
re the last of the old professional fishing families. Fishing has
een synonymous with Encounter Bay since the beginning of the
ıst century when the whalers came, and it was all done the hard
ay with oars, manpower and flat bottom boats.

he original Malen Rumbelow and his family arrived from Suffolk in
ıe "Pestonjee Bomanjee" in 1854. The first Ewens arrived from
Jlasgow in Scotland around the same time. Alec, the grandfather of
ill and George was the last Manager of the Bluff Whaling Station
·om 1871-1878. The Shannons arrived on the "Solway" and the
South Australian". George Shannon bought land at Waitpinga in
842, his son Jos later becoming a professional fisherman, a calling
arried on by his grandsons, Lin and Murray, who today are still
shing—but only for pleasure.

hoto *(top left)* pictures the present Malen Rumbelow with the
at-bottom boat he uses so effectively. *(Lower left)* Lin and Murray
hannon. *(Above)* Bill Ewen is seen with his fishing mate "Pelican
ill". *(Overleaf)* George Ewen pauses to gauge the temper of the sea
e has known and loved all his life.

FORMER HARBORMASTER'S RESIDENCE, CUSTOMS HOUSE AND STATIONMASTER'S RESIDENCE

H.J. BAKER 1989

Situated close to the causeway to Granite Island and in the hub of old Port Victor, this building was commenced in 1866 with additions in 1878.

Built in the Georgian style, the house had a slate roof and has seven main rooms and a cellar.

An interesting feature is the outside toilet built on for the night cart era.

Use of the house for the Harbormaster and Collector of Customs reflects the importance of Port Victor, mainly for export purposes by overseas sailing ships.

With the demise of shipping, the property was acquired by the South Australian Railways in 1911 and used as the Stationmaster's residence for almost 60 years.

Awaiting permanent transfer, the Victor Harbor Branch of the National Trust of SA has rented the premises from the District Council of Victor Harbor since 1986.

The building is currently called the Old Customs and Stationmaster's House and operates as a museum. It is now on the State Heritage Register.

Supplement to "180 Years of Victor Harbor History" by J. Bartlett.
Compiled by the Victor Harbor Branch of the National Trust of SA.

must down to the seas again, for the call of the running tide
  Is a wild call and a clear call that may not be denied:
nd all I ask is a windy day with the white clouds flying,
   And the flung spray and the blown spume, and the sea-gulls crying.

John Masefield

Thank-you page

Mr. Ainslie Roberts, who designed this book, and also spent many weeks creating order out of a mountain of chaos in order to do so. As part-time residents of Encounter Bay for eighteen years, he and his wife Melva Jean have also contributed much material gained from their own research into local Heritage.

Mrs. Hazel Zilm, who has contributed a wealth of information and has given much guidance and encouragement.

Rev. John Cameron, who has unearthed for us much valuable material, and who has given so fully of his knowledge.

The 'Victor Harbor Times', who have been part of Victor Harbor for 70 years. They showed enthusiasm for our project and much tolerance with our delvings and borrowings, and readily allowed us to use many of their photographs in this book.

The South Australian Archives who, had they not been this State's first Heritage-conscious body, would not be in a position to help us as they have done.

Mr Peter Cotton of Gillingham Printers, whose enthusiasm and personal involvement in this project carried him far beyond the bounds of commercial duty.

Mrs Margaret Page, who generously denuded the walls of her Coffee Shop for the weeks necessary to reproduce so many of the photographs which appear in this book.

Thank you to Reg. Arnold, John B. Blanden, Department of Lands, Rex Elliot, Olwen Henderson, Bert Puxley, Gary Roberts, Kel Roberts Gwen Rumbelow, Shirley Rumbelow, Royal Automobile Association of S.A., R. T. Sexton, Nancy Sibley, Neville Solly, State Library of S.A., Rex and Dorothy Tilbrook, Ken Tregenza, Faye White.

Jeanette Bartlett